"OF LOVE AND LIFE"

OTHER BOOKS BY ROBERT M. DRAKE

Spaceship (2012)
The Great Artist (2012)
Science (2013)
Beautiful Chaos (2014)
Beautiful Chaos 2 (2014)
Black Butterfly (2015)
A Brilliant Madness (2015)
Beautiful and Damned (2016)
Broken Flowers (2016)
Gravity: A Novel (2017)
Star Theory (2017)
Chaos Theory (2017)
Light Theory (2017)
Moon Theory (2017)
Dead Pop Art (2017)
Chasing The Gloom: A Novel (2017)
Moon Matrix (2018)
Seeds of Wrath (2018)
Dawn of Mayhem (2018)
The King is Dead (2018)
What I Feel When I Don't Want To Feel (2019)
What I Say To Myself When I Need To Calm The Fuck Down (2019)
What I Say When I'm Not Saying A Damn Thing (2019)
What I Mean When I Say Miss You, Love You & Fuck You (2019)
What I Say To Myself When I Need To Walk Away, Let Go And Fucking Move On (2019)
What I Really Mean When I Say Good-bye, Don't Go And Leave Me The Fuck Alone (2019)
The Advice I Give Others But Fail To Practice My Damn Self (2019)
The Things I Feel In My Fucking Soul And The Things That Took Years To Understand (2019)
Something Broken, Something Beautiful Vol 1 (2020)
Something Broken, Something Beautiful Vol 2 (2020)
Something Broken, Something Beautiful Vol 3 (2021)
Chasing Moons & Rainbows (2021)
I WROTE THIS FOR YOU ME AND ANYONE TRYING TO FUCKING MOVE ON (2021)
BUT IN THE END YOU JUST HAVE TO LET GO (2022)
OF LOVE AND LIFE (2022)
LOVE STORIES SUCK! (2023)
A BEAUTIFUL MIND (2023)

For Excerpts and Updates please follow:

Instagram.com/rmdrk
Facebook.com/rmdrk
Twitter.com/rmdrk
Tiktok.com/rmdrk
Tumblr.com/rmdrk
Snapchat.com/rmdrk

Book Cover: ROBERT M. DRAKE

For the broken For the beautiful
You know who you are

From the Author:

Sometimes I feel like I am breaking apart. I don't know what is happening to me. I can't remember. I can't focus. I can't spell. Most days I feel like I am living in a dream. As if everything around me is not real. I feel like I am making this up as it goes. My life is not my life. Or so it seems to me. This world is a figment of my own imagination. I'm trying to hold on to my memories. To my friends. To my family. To my readers. It just gets to hard sometimes. The errors. The mistakes. The things I wish I could take back and redo. Not just in love but in life as well. I am breaking apart. And I just hope someone familiar is there with me to collect the pieces. To help me put them back together again. I just hope, in the end, I am not alone.

"OF LOVE AND LIFE"

WHEN YOU FIND SOMEONE YOU LOVE AND THEY MADE A HOME UNDER YOUR SKIN

We all have
that one person

we wish
we could have held onto

a little longer.

That one person
we wish

could have stayed.

The one
we go back to
and wonder

how different
things

could have been

if only

we had met at a better
more stable

moment
in our lives.

The one *that* got away.

The one
that never made it out

of our hearts.

The one we wish
we could have stayed

with

forever.

WHEN IT HURTS WE ALL RELATE AND WHEN IT DOES NOT WE CAN ALL REMEMBER WHAT IT WAS LIKE

We fell in love
at a very strange time

in our lives.

And oddly enough
we let go

too soon.

And this
is now the story

of our lives.

WHEN THERE IS NOTHING LEFT TO SAY OR DO, THEN WHAT MUST BE DONE NEXT IS COMPLETELY UP TO YOU

It's okay
to walk away.

Especially
when you feel exhausted

and feel
like you have nothing

left to give.

It's okay
to choose yourself

sometimes.

It's okay
to let *it all* go.

THE BRUTAL FATE OF THINGS AND THE HONEST TRUTH OF WHAT HAPPENS AFTER

Honestly

I didn't want
the attention.

I didn't need it.

I just wanted you
to love me.

To be there for me.

To show me that
there are still some good people

out there.

I wanted your kindness.
Your patience.

Your trust.

I just wanted your heart.
And like all good things it came to an end

too soon.

Too soon.

Things end too soon.

Childhood ends too soon.
Ideas end too soon.

Patience ends too soon.
Life ends too soon.

Fires in the soul end too soon.
Inspiration ends too soon.

And so on…

And then
there is you…

And our love
too

ended too soon.

Like everything else.

I wish things could have been different though... I wish things weren't shaped like everything else.

WHEN THE STING CARRYS OVER THE STING IS THERE TO REMIND YOU OF THE PAST

I felt you
in my soul.

And that's why
I reacted

the way I reacted.

But you came
and I let you stay.

And then
you left

and I let you go.

And to be honest,
that was one

of the hardest things

I ever

had to do.
But I did and I overcame.

And I learned
that after you

there was another life.

Another love.
Another plan.

Another world.

But it wasn't the same.

Nothing
is ever truly the same.

And that
is where

that ends.

HOW SELF-LOVE CAN SAVE YOU AND HOW IT WILL CHANGE YOUR LIFE FOREVER

Sometimes
the *true love*

everyone always talks about

is the self-love
you have for yourself.

You just have
to put the time you need

on yourself
and remember

that
you too
are a person.

That
you too

have your own needs.

Wants.
Desires.

You have to love yourself
and sometimes that means

putting the whole world aside
and focusing

only on you.

Let this be your mantra.

Let this be
the first thing

you think about
every morning.

This is your life
and everything should revolve

around you
and nothing else.

Amen!

There is nothing like self-love.

—

WHEN YOUR SKIN IS MADE OF STONE THE GHOST OF YOUR PAST CANNOT LINGER

Maybe that's
when your healing begins.

The moment you realize
they can't hurt you

anymore.

The moment anything
they say

or do

can't get under your skin.

WHEN YOU HAVE A THRONE IN THE SUN YOU ARE LIGHT AND YOU ARE WIND COMBINED

You can care for them
and still keep

your distance.

You can move on from them
and still be kind.

Just because
they hurt you

doesn't mean
you must hurt them.

Know your place in the universe.
Know your path.

You are *not* like them.

You are different.
You are special.

You know it.
You feel it.

You
are
so
much
more!

WHEN YOU STILL CARE FOR THEM
IT IS OKAY TO WISH THEM WELL

I still care for you.

Although
we are no longer
together.

I still want
you to succeed.

To live a life
you can be proud of.

I still want you
to find happiness.

To find
what makes you smile.

What makes you laugh.
To find the moments

that speak to you.

That take your breath away.

We aren't together
 but I still want these things

for you.

Because I'm that kind of person.
I cared for you that much.

And I just want
the goodness of life

to touch you.
To be with you.

Even if
you are not with me.

HOW FAR IS TOO FAR?

Distance.

A funny little thing.

Because although
it can heal you

it can also
tear you apart.

IT COULD BE TOMORROW IT
COULD BE FIVE MAYBE TEN YEARS
FROM NOW BUT ONE DAY IT WILL
ALL MAKE SENSE

Maybe one day
when we are older

we will accidentally
run into each other

and apologize
for all the trouble

we might have caused.

Or maybe one day
we will find each other

and sit
silently

across one another

and for the first time...

finally understand

how it all went wrong.
It will all make sense
in that small
little instance.

You will know
and I will know

that in the end,
it was all

for the best.

OF LIFE AND OF LOVE AND OF STARDUST AND OTHER THINGS THST MAKE US FEEL WHAT WE FEEL

It's not
that we were bad

for each other.

It's just
we were too immature

to understand
that good communication

was all
it took

to make things work.
To make things last.

To make each other
want to stay.

That's love.
That's live.

And somewhere in-between
that's us.

THE EYES CARRY A TRUTH NO ONE CAN EVER REVEAL THAT IS IF YOU ARE NOT PAYING ATTENTION

It's in the eyes.

Pay attention
to her eyes.

They say it all.

They'll let you know
how she really feels.

WHEN YOUR STORY PLAYS OUT THE WAY YOU DID NOT WANT IT TO, DO NOT WORRY THE UNIVERSE HAS A BETTER PLAN

I know how you feel.

As if everyone
you have ever loved

has left you.

But that's not true.

The only ones
who have left you

have been the assholes
who didn't deserve you.

The ones who didn't know
how to love you.

The ones who took you
for granted.

Life is about perspective.

And not all things
are what they seem.

Everything happens for a reason.

Your whole life unfolds
the way

it was meant
to unfold.

Every crease.
Every wrinkle.

Every thought.
Every feeling.

Everything is meant
and designed to bring you closer

to whom
you are really meant

to be.

That's all.

WHEN THE SIGNS ARE EVERYWHERE PLEASE TAKE THEM FOR WHAT THEY ARE

In order
to make the relationship work

all you have to do
is listen.

Communicate.

And be honest
with one another.

That's the secret.

That's all it'll take
to make it last.

Forever.

WHEN YOU CHANGE FOR LOVE
YOU CHANGE FOR GOOD

It's okay
to change for someone.

Sometimes sacrifice is needed
to make things work.

To make things last.

It's okay
to change for someone.

That is,
if it's what you want.

If it's what
you believe in.

It's only okay
to do so

or love.

For a chance
to be loved.

And not for anything else.

Change for love.
For hope.

For all things that speak
to your heart.

Change is inevitable.

HOW CAN YOU THINK YOU ARE WEAK WHEN EVERYTIME YOU FALL YOU COME BACK STRONGER

You choose
who to love.

NEVER forget that.

No matter what they say
it is you

who chooses
who to let in.

It is you
who chooses

who to let out.

Who to hold onto.
Who to fight for.

Who to move on from.

And who to leave
behind.
This is your life.
This is your heart.

Never forget
it is you

who is in *control*
and no one else.

You decide
how you want to spend

the rest of your life.
You get to choose

who to love.

Who to live for
even if it is for yourself.

WHEN YOU START OVER YOU START FOR THE BEST AND YOU START FOR YOURSELF AND NO ONE ELSE

So you got
your heart broken.

Well,
we all do sometimes.

But you know what
you're alive

and you're going to get
a new day

and start over.

Face what hurts.
Deal with the pain.

Day by day.
Night by night.

One step at a time.

Because you're a fighter, baby.
You know it.
I know it.

The world knows it.

And this heartache
isn't going to stop you.

It's going
to make you stronger.

This is only
the beginning of all the things

you're meant
to feel.

WHEN YOU WANT TO MOVE OUT TO MOVE INTO ANOTHER PERSONS SOUL YOU BECOME A STAR YOU BECOME A FLOWER IN THE SOIL OF OTHER PEOPLE

Allow yourself
to be loved.

So you can experience
what it is like

to make a home
out of

another person.

ACTIONS WILL ALWAYS SHOW YOU HOW MUCH THEY CARE AND THEY WILL MAKE YOU REALIZE IF IT IS WORTH SAVING

He's trying
to fix his mistakes.

Trying
to correct his past

behavior.

Let him show you
how much he cares.

How much
he really wants

to make it work.

We all make mistakes.
Let him love you.

Let him show you

how much

you mean to him.
He doesn't want
to lose you.

He's not ready
to let go.

He's ready to work
on the relationship.

Ready to work
on himself.

Ready to save
what he loves.

BUT remember,
let him show you

with his actions
and ***not***

with his words.

**WHEN ANOTHER PERSON SHOWS
YOU THE WAY AND YOU FOLLOW
AND YOU END UP FINDING MORE
THAN THAT OF WHAT YOU
BELIEVE IN**

Maybe that's
what you need.

The love
of another person.

Sometimes
that's all it takes

to make
things feel real.

WHEN THE SUN STAYS OUT TOO LONG YOU TOO BECOME A PART OF THE LIGHT

Sweet love
it's all in your head.

The anxiety
you feel

starts there.

Take a break.

Breathe
and recollect your thoughts
and feelings.

You got this.

Don't let your fears
take control

of your heart
of your life.

You are enough
and you will always
ALWAYS have the sun

on your side.

WHEN YOU FINALLY UNDERSTAND
THE WORLD JUST SETTLES
BETWEEN YOUR HANDS

That's the thing.

You think
you want to be

alone.

You think
no one really cares.

And you think
maybe love

is full of shit.

But it's not.
You just want

to be loved.

Held.

You just want
to feel appreciated.

Needed.

All you really want
is someone

who understands.

WHEN YOU SURRENDER YOURSELF
EVERYTHING IS BEAUTIFUL

Everything will fall
into place

the moment you stop
trying

to control
every fucking little thing.

Every fucking little detail.
.
Let your life flow.

Trust
what the universe has

for you.

WHEN YOU REAS A POEM IN A BOOK AND IT JUST CONNECTS AND MAKES PERFECT SENSE

Slow down.

You don't have
to rush through

e v e r y t h i n g.

Take your time on people.
On yourself.

Be patient with them.
With everything

you do.

Social media
has placed us

in this fast-paced world.

But

life doesn't have
to be this way.

We can be patient
with each other.

And with ourselves.

We can take
time off

to only pick up right
where we left off.

What I'm trying to say is
we don't need

to fall in love
right away.

We have
our entire lives

ahead of us
for that.

WHEN YOU REALLY CARE THAT IS ALL

I don't care
about your accolades.

About your career.
About how many different

countries
you've visited.

I don't care
if you're popular.

Or

if you're the smartest
person in the room.

I don't care
about how much money

you have.

What type of clothes
you're wearing

or

what type of car
you drive.

All I care about
is

if you're truly happy with yourself.
If you're happy

with your life.

I just want
you to live a life

you're proud of.

And if the love you
have within has grown within.

I hope this makes sense to you.
That's all.

WHEN YOU OPEN YOURSELF UP YOU BLOOM LIKE A FLOWER AND GROW LIKE A TREE

People
would feel better

about themselves

if they did
everything

with a little
love.

WHEN LIFE GETS TO COMPLICATED LOOK INWARD ALL THE ANSWERS ARE THERE

Maybe it's not
about being loved

by another human.

Maybe
it's all about loving
yourself.

Loving who you are.
Who you could be.

And maybe

that's

what matters most.

HOW TIME WORKS WITH YOU TO SHOW YOU WHO TO KEEP AND WHO TO LET GO

I know
it hurts right now.

But you will
outgrow them.

You will see.

How we all
Eventually

learn to let go
of all the people

we once thought
we could *never*

live without.

Just give it time.
And give yourself

the love you deserve.
Time will show you many things.

It will show you
who is real

and who
is not.

WHEN THE HEART IS FULL OF ROOMS YOU AND ONLY YOU HOLD THE MASTER KEY

You are *not*
too complicated to love.

It is just

you haven't found
the right person.

You haven't found
someone

who understands.

Who speaks the same
language as you.

Don't ever feel convinced
that you are

too hard
to love

because of this.
You are unique.

And not everyone
will get that.

Not everyone
is meant

to understand
all of the things

that are constantly going on
in your heart.

WHEN YOUR BESTFRIEND IS MORE THAN JUST A BESTFRIEND THEY BECOME YOUR SOULMATE

Sometimes
your soulmate manifests

in the form
of a friend.

Sometimes that's what you get.

And there is
absolutely

nothing
wrong
with
that.

WITH TIME YOU WILL SEE HOW SOME PEOPLE ARE MEANT TO BE HELD A LITTLE LONGER THAN OTHERS

With time
you will see.

How it is always
the right ones

who never leave.

How it is always
the right ones

who stand by your side
when you need them

most.

Those who make
the effort.

Who want the relationship

to grow.

To flourish
into something beautiful.

With time.

You will see.
And realize this.

You will appreciate the lessons learned
from those who left.

But you will *ALWAYS*
be grateful for the blessings

earned from those
who've stayed.

Sometimes
there is nothing

more beautiful
than that.

WHEN YOU FLY YOU FALL AND THEN YOU FLY AGAIN LIFE BECOMES SO PRECIOUS THAN THE AIR

Maybe one day
we will let go

of all the bullshit
that caused us

to separate
from each other.

And maybe one day
we will finally learn

how
to be free.

WHEN YOU HAVE HAD ENOUGH BUT DO NOT KNOW HOW OR WHERE TO BEGIN YOU LOOK WITHIN AND SOMETIMES YOU LOOK FOR A FRIEND

I didn't need
a therapist.

I just needed some time
to myself.

Time to get away.

From the chaos.
From the anxieties

life brought.

From all the things
that brought out the darkness.

That's all
I really needed.

Time.

To recollect.
To reflect.
To grow.

And somewhere in between.

I just needed your support.
That's all.

Sometimes the support
of someone you love

is all you need
to get out

of the darkness.

And sometimes
that's all

we have.

WHEN YOU DO THINGSA FOR YOURSELF YOU WILL SEE HOW SPECIAL THINGS TURN OUT TO BE

Don't do it for them.
Do it for you.

You don't need
to prove

anything to anyone
other than yourself.

So let them doubt you.

Let them think
what they want.

And don't let them
control

what you feel.

Don't let them
get a hold of you

this way.

Do it for you.

Whatever it may be.
Do it

because you deserve it.
And not because

they think you can't.

Everything you do
should be in benefit

to yourself
and not

to impress others.

Not to get
the validation

of people
you don't need.

Of people
who don't

give a damn about you.

Do it all for you.
Always for you.

AMEN!

WHEN THE WORLD ENDS YOU FIND A WAY TO SURVIVE YOU FIND A WAY TO BREATHE

There's no
easy way to say it.

But in the end,
it was I

who loved the most.

It was I
who was willing

to go through hell
and back

for you.

For us.
It was I

who really wanted it
to work out.

That wanted us
to stay.

To be together.
No matter what.

But that was foolish of me.

That is not
how it unfolded.

You left
and I stayed.

I stayed where we met.

Stayed where
we first kissed.

Where we first
held hands.

Where we first
said to each other

we would always

be together.
I believed you.

And I stayed where I thought
you would always be.

I'm sorry for everything.
I hope one day

I find you
to tell you

how much
I miss you.

WHEN YOUR HEART DRIVES THE CAR YOU JUST SIT BACK AND ENJOY THE JOURNEY

Stop waiting
for the right time.

Start now.

Do it now.
Love now.

Tell them how
you feel.

Right now.

There is no
perfect moment.

There is only now
and what you do

with the time
you have *right now.*

Don't waste
another moment not living

the way you want.
Not telling them
how you feel.

Not chasing
what makes you free.

You are not here
forever.

The right time is here.
And the right time

is now!

Sometimes you just
have to take that risk.

Be vulnerable.

Let go of your fears
and say it.

Open the doors
and flow.

Your heart
will lead the way.

THIS WILL ONLY MAKE SENSE TO A FEW BUT SOMETIMES THIS IS JUST THE WAY IT IS

That's life.

Sometimes you find
someone you love.

And sometimes
you lose them.

They become your everything.
And sometimes you lose

everything
when they're gone.

WHEN THEY THINK YOU WANT THEM BACK THEY ARE DEAD WRONG

I don't want
you back.

I just want
every piece of me

I gave you.

All the love.
All the time.

All the attention.

All the dedication
and all the moments

I could have given
to someone else.

That's
what I want.

THIS BOOK IS MORE ABOUT FRIENDSHIP THAN ANYTHING ELSE PLEASE TAKE A LOOK CLOSER

That's the thing
about friendships.

Sometimes
they can make you

forget the pain.

And sometimes
they can make you

remember.

And that
within itself

is

a beautiful thing.

Maybe
I have always been

a fool.

Because I believe
too much

in people.

In love.
In communication.
In honesty.

Or maybe
I'm just too naive

to realize
how some people

are only in it
for themselves.

WHEN THE WORLD IS FULL OF ASSHOLES AND YOU FEEL LIKE THE ONLY PERSON WITH A HEART

I understand

that everyone
is always looking

for a way out.

But I don't understand
how some

not all
are *only*

and always thinking
about themselves.

I guess we live
in a world

full of assholes.

And I guess
I'm just

another sucker
who believes

in the goodness
we all can

bring.

Sometimes I'm a dreamer
and sometimes

I believe too much
in the human heart.

I CANNOT FOR THE LIFE OF ME!

I don't understand
some of these men.

If you say
she's a keeper.

Then *FUCKING*
keep her!

And stop
treating her like shit.

WHEN YOU ARE TOO AFRAID TO SHOW WHAT YOU FEEL THERE COMES A TIME WHEN IT IS THE ONLY THING TO DO

It's simple.

Just show them
you care

without having
to say it.

Show them
you need them.

Show them
how much they mean

to you.

All else means nothing.
A relationship will flourish

with honesty

and action.

With communication.
Just show it.

Don't hide it.
Don't hold on

to your feelings.

Let them go.
The other person *will*

appreciate this.

They will hold on
to the things you DO

in their hearts.
Forever.

This…
is the only way.

WHEN YOU ARE TOO AFRAID TO SHOW WHAT YOU FEEL THERE COMES A TIME WHEN IT IS THE ONLY THING TO DO PT 2

All the things
you say

mean nothing.

Not unless
you put some *action*
into it.

So if you say
you want things

to work out
then make them

work out.

Do what you must.
Sacrifice what you must.

If you say
you want to be together

then let's be together.
Just be honest.

Let's give each other
space

when needed.

Let's give each other
time.

Patience.
Loyalty.
Respect.

And if you say
you love me

then by all means,
please

just fucking love me.

With all your heart.
With all your soul.

With everything you can.

Love me.
Love me deeply.

And I'll make sure
you know how I feel too.

With action.
Not with words.

Love me!

And do it
because doing anything else

wouldn't make much sense.
At all.

READ THIS AGAIN THEN AGAIN AND AGAIN TIL IT IS SOMETHING YOU JUST DO NATURALLY

You'll never
be happy

with yourself
if you don't

follow

all the things
you feel.

ONE DAY IS JUST A DAY AWAY SO PLEASE BE KIND TO YOURSELF

One day
everything that broke you

will make sense.

And you will know
why it happened

the way
it happened

and at what cost

and why it hurt
the way it hurt.

WHEN YOU GIVE AND GIVE YOU THINK YOU HAVE NOTHING LEFT BUT IN REALITY YOU DO YOU WILL ALWAYS HAVE A LITTLE MORE LEFT

Yes,
you gave
a piece

of your soul

to the wrong one.
But you still

have your life
ahead of you.

And soon enough,
the right one

will find you.
And make everything

you lost

with your prior
relationship

seem
like it was nothing

at all.

WHEN YOU KNOW YOU JUST KNOW AND NOTHING CAN STOP YOU FEROM THIS POINT ON

I know you don't
like being alone.

But you have to
stop stressing it.

You have to
stop forcing things

to happen.

A new relationship
will bloom

when you least
expect it.

You just have
to stop

trying to control

everything.
And accept
the way

things are.
And let

things happen
as they should.

At their place.

Pace.
And time.

And when the universe
decides

you are ready,

you will be ready!
Amen.

THE MOST IMPORTANT DAY OF YOUR LIFE WILL CHANGE YOUR LIFE FOREVER

The most
important day

of your life
is not the day

you get married.

Or the day
you graduate from college

or the day
you land your first

real job.

No.
The most important day
of your life

is the day

you realize

your self-worth.

The day you realize
that you are enough.

Not only for the world
but also

for yourself.

The day you realize
that the love

you have
for yourself...

is the strongest
kind of love there is.

The one that starts
with you.

The one you share
with other people.

The one you've always
had within.

That is the *most*
important day of your life.

Realizing your self-love.
And knowing

how irreplaceable
you truly are.

SOMETIMES YOU SAY GOOD-BYE TO THE PEOPLE YOU LOVE AND SOMETIMES YOU HOLD ON TO THOSE YOU WANT TO LET GO THAT IS LIFE

Saying goodbye
is never easy.

No matter who decides
to say it first.

No matter who decides
to move on.

We are built
to stay

with those
we love.

No matter how toxic
things get.

We are designed

to be together.

To stay connected.

The thing is,
hope is naturally

embedded
in our souls.

We are destined
to try

to make things work.
To give chances.

No matter how many times
we've been broken.

*We want to love
to the very end.*

But there comes a time
when you must

decide.

A time of life
and death.

Of choosing what's right
for you

over what's wrong.

The light
over the darkness.

There comes a time
when enough

is enough.

In other words.
No matter how much love

you've given them.

It is in our hearts
to choose

what's right for us.

To choose life.
To choose the light.

To choose the people
who want to stay.

Who want to love.
To share.

To grow.
To inspire.

We want to be happy.
All of us.

It is just…
sometimes to learn
to appreciate life…

we must
go through some

of the darkness moments.

And some bad
experiences

will teach you this.

So don't feel too bad
for saying goodbye.

For choosing
your own happiness

and mental health
over them.

You are designed
to love others

but also
designed to love yourself.

And that
should *never.*

Ever.
Change.

No matter who
you fall in love with.

No matter who
decides to stay

or not.

WHEN YOU MEET TOO MANY PEOPLE AND MOST OF THEM ARE A BUNCH OF ASSHOLES

If someone
is confused

whether to be with you
or not

then
don't fall into

that game.

You are not
someone's second choice.

Not
someone's maybe.

Or what if.
Or *"I'm not sure."*

You don't deserve that,

baby girl.

Believe me
when I say,

you are way too beautiful
for that mess.

And mixed signals
are for assholes.

You deserve someone
who knows

exactly
what they want.

WHEN IT HURTS IT JUST HURTS BUT WITH TIME IT WILL HEAL AND IT WILL NOT LINGER AS IT ONCE DID TRUST THIS

There will be
moments of agony.

Moments of pain
and tears.

Of sadness.

But I hope
when those moments pass…

I hope
you find it within
yourself

to move on.

To take the lessons
you learned

and start over.

I hope you find
the strength
you need to put

all of those things
that once hurt you

behind you.

And I hope you
learn to take things easy.

To not let everything
affect you.

To not let
the people who don't care

get under your skin.

I hope you find it
within yourself

to let

things go.

To not live
with all that heaviness.

To not hold things
within.

Grudges.
Regret.

Things that pull you deeper
into the void.

I hope you realize
that sometimes

it is okay
to be alone.

To choose yourself
over others.

To want to get away.

Start over

without telling
a single person.

In these hard moments
I hope

you find it within yourself
to make things softer.

To be kinder
to yourself

when you need it most.

To take a step back
and reflect

when you feel
as if

you are in the center
of the chaos.

The one
only the world
can bring.

I hope you realize
your magic.

Your value.

Your potential
and how some of these

hard moments
will test you.

They will put you
on the edge.

They will force you
to decide

whether to choose greatness
or anguish.

To choose to love
or to live

in pain.

I hope you understand

that these moments
will not be easy.

They will be
some of your hardest.

Some of your most
difficult

to get through.

But they will pass.
You will get over them.

And I hope
what you take

from them
helps set you free.

I hope
they give you wings.

And I hope
you choose to fly.

In a world
that is designed

to pull you under
and make you fall.

I hope you stay
above the clouds.

NOBODY SAID IT WAS EASY BUT ALSO NOBODY SAID IT WAS GOING TO BE SO HARD

You have to
move on

from your past,
my love.

I know
it is a hard thing

to do.

But you have to
start somewhere.

You have to
take it day by day.

Hour by hour.
Minute by minute.

You have to.

You can't

start your process
and then go back

to them
and expect things

to be okay.

That's not
how it works.

You have to be serious
about your future.

Serious
about leaving the bullshit behind.

Serious
about starting over.

You have to.

And it's not easy.
Believe me I know.

And no one ever said
that the process

was going to be.

But you have to start somewhere.

And everyday
you have to take

the same steps.
The same precautions.

And have the same level
of awareness.

You have to know
that this

is… indeed
a part of your process.

That this is
the only way.

You will learn
how to move on from them.

From all the relationships
that do more harm

than good.

You have to know
that some days

you will be weaker
than others.

That--that
is expected to happen.

But you have to start
somewhere.

You have to
surround yourself

with your friends.
Your family.

Do things
that'll keep you busy

from going back to them.

And soon enough,
you will see.

As the days
turn to weeks

and the weeks
turn to months.

You will see
how not having them around

won't bother you
anymore.

You will see
how much better

your life will be.
How much relief

you will feel
when you give

yourself the time
you need to heal.

You will also realize
how your process

was worth it.
Was necessary.

And not to mention,
you will be thankful

for all the bad relationships.
You will be

appreciative
of all the pain

they've caused.

Because
it will allow you

these rare
special moments

of reflection.

Moments to recognize
what you do

and don't deserve.

You have to move on
from your past,

my love.

You just have
to find it within

yourself
to start somewhere.

Find it within
yourself

to want
to heal.

To want
to get over

the people who hurt you.
And want

to actually
move on.

WHEN YOU FIND THE RIGHT PEOPLE YOU WILL FEEL IT IN YOUR BONES

The right people
will love you

differently.

And you won't have
to second guess it

or question it.

You'll just know.
It'll be that real.

It'll be that deep.

WHEN YOU LET GO OF THE PEOPLE YOU LOVE IT IS A GOOD FEELING TO GIVE THEM THEIR WINGS

It's okay
if you want to go.

I don't blame you
for wanting more.

I just hope
you find yourself.

And I hope
you realize

how here
with me

you will always
have a home.

Just don't be gone
for too long.

I will miss you.

And I will remember you
for all

the beautiful memories
you gave me.

SOMETIMES GOOD ADVICE IS BAD ADVICE AND BAD ADVICE IS GOOD ADVICE

Sometimes
ignoring them

does more harm
than good.

I just hope
you know the difference.

And when to use it
to make a statement.

To prove a point.

And not because
you want

to get back at them.

Not because
you want

to hurt them

just as bad
as they hurt you.

That will not
heal your pain.

It will only
bring the darkness closer

than that
of what

it really is.

SOMETIMES ONLY SOMETIMES

Sometimes
your perspective changes.

And sometimes
it's you

and not
the people you love.

Sometimes
you just outgrow them.

Sometimes
you just want more.

Sometimes
your soul

just demands a change.
Demands a new job.

New people.
New places

to find yourself in.

And that doesn't
make you

a bad person.

And it doesn't
mean

you don't care
about them.

It just means
you've changed.

You've outgrown
your space.

And it is both
as simple

and as complicated
as that.

WHEN YOUR FRIEND IS THERE FOR YOU EVERYTHING IS GOING TO BE OKAY

You stayed with me.
To help me.

To save me.
To go through it.

With me.

And although nothing changed.
You came.

And only
because of me.

And that's all
that matters.

That fact that you tried.
That you really

gave it your all.

And you showed me
how much
you cared.

To me...
that's what

friendship
is all about.

To have someone
who's going to be there

for you.

No matter what
the outcome is.

A friend
is someone
who stays.

Who believes
in the greater good.

Who gives you light.

Hope.

Even when
there is

very little
to go around.

WHEN YOU DO NOT NEED A REASON TO SHOW SOMEONE YOU CARE YOU BECOME A PART OF THEIR GROWTH

You don't need
a reason

to want to be
good to someone.

To want
to save someone.

To want
to watch someone grow.

You don't need
an explanation for that

either.

Some people
just don't get it.

They don't
understand
the importance of friendship.

Of unity.
Of forming relationships

that'll last
a lifetime.

Of going out
of your way

for someone.

Some people
are just lost.

They just don't care
about

other people.

They do
or rather

don't do
things to let others know

how much
they care.

WHEN YOU TRY AND TRY BUT NOTHING SEEMS TO WORK THEN PERHAPS IT IS NOT MEANT TO BE

No matter
how many chances

you give them

you never really
come back

together
the same way.

WHEN YOU FEEL IT IN YOUR GUT THEN THE FEELING IT USUALLY RIGHT

You'll know
how much they care...

by what
they are willing

to go through
for you.

IT TAKES COURAGE AND GUTS TO GET OVER SOMEONE TO MOVE ON FROM SOMEONE AND LET GO

It takes
a lot of self-love

to get over
the hardest situations.

To get over
the hardest

relationships—people.

WHEN YOU BECOME AN EMPATH
EVERYTHING IS IMPORTANT

Just because
it doesn't affect you

doesn't mean
it doesn't affect others.

We all take
similar situations

differently.

We must always remember
to be kind.

To be graceful.
To be understanding

and gentle.

Always.

We all need that "grow together" type of love.

It is never too late to start over.

WHEN YOU START OVER AND THINGS BEGIN TO FEEL FAMILIAR

It took
everything out of you

to heal.

To get over
your past.

But don't be afraid
to love again.

To get hurt again.

To take the risk.
Again and again and again.

You're a lot stronger
than you think.

WHEN LOVE STORIES SUCK BUT WE CAN STILL READ POETRY TOGETHER

"I'm afraid of love.
After what I just went through.

I don't think
I can take it

anymore.

It's not worth it for me,"
she said.

"Please don't say that.
Don't believe that.

Don't shut your heart
because of someone's

carelessness.

You deserve it.

You deserve love.

It's just you fell in love
with the wrong person.

But there is
someone out there

for you.

Someone who's willing
to give you

what you need.
What you deserve.

Someone like you.

Who's been through hell.
Who knows what it's

like to be cut
deeper than any wound possible.

It hurts.

I know.

But closing your heart
isn't the answer.

It just isn't.

Keep it open.

Always leave
a little room inside

for someone new.

Stay strong,
my sweet friend.

Soon enough,
it will all unfold

and you will be
where you want to be."

WHEN YOU KNOW YOU ARE ENOUGH BUT STILL LISTEN TO THE THINGS ASSHOLES TELL YOU! DO NOT BELIEVE THEM

You. Are. Not.

Too complicated to love.

*Don't believe
the bullshit*

people tell you.

WHEN YOU CHANGE BUT REMEMBER WHAT IT FELT LIKE TO BE IN LOVE WITH SOMEONE THAT KIND OF MEMORY STAYS WITH YOU FOREVER

No one ever stays
the same.

People change.

It is just…
sometimes…

you will change too.
I will change.

We all will change.

Eventually.
And then we wonder

how it happened.

Why some people

don't feel the same.

Don't move us
the same.
Don't speak to us
the same.

Don't care the same.

People change
and that's one thing

that doesn't change.

It is inevitable.
And when we change

because we will
I just want you

to remember…

how much
I loved you.

I just want you

to remember

that in this
very moment
I was willing
to be with you

forever.

In every aspect
and in every sense.

*I WANTED
TO BE WITH YOU.*

STAY WITH YOU.

FOREVER.

WHEN OVERTHINKING BECOMES MORE THAN OVERTHINKING YOU BECOME A WALKING PROBLEM

I know it's easier
said

than done

but you have to
control

all of that
overthinking

you've been doing lately.

You're creating scenarios
that don't exist.

And that's how
you're breaking

your own heart,
love.

That's why it hurts.

That's why sometimes
you drive yourself

mad.

WHEN YOUR ARMS BECOME PILLOWS AND YOUR PILLOWS BECOME A RESTING PLACE FOR SOMEONE YOU LOVE

I know
you're exhausted.

And I know
you have

to keep going.

Keep fighting
for what you love.

But why don't you
come here

and rest
for a while.

Why don't you
take a break.

I am here.
And I am your home.

And I just don't want
you to overexert

yourself.

I know you're strong, baby.

But it's okay
to lay your heart

on my palm.

I know it's heavy.
And I know

how stressed you've been.

Come lay with me.
Take your mind off things.

And breathe.

I just want you to know

that I got you.

Sometimes
you have to carry

the people
you love.

And comfort them.

Let them know
they are safe.

Let them know
things
will be okay.

WHEN THEY RUNAWAY FROM HOME LET THEM BE IF THEY COME BACK THEY ARE YOURS IF NOT THEY WERE NEVER YOURS TO BEGIN WITH

People
are going to walk away.

But it is
your absolute duty

not
to follow them

if they do.

You should never hold on
to anyone

who doesn't
want to stay.

THE END.

WHEN YOUR SCARS SPEAK BACK
TO YOU THEY SPEAK THE TRUTH
IN THE HARSHEST OF WAYS

You don't have
to chase them.

You don't have
to apologize.

You don't have
to try to convince them

to stay.

You didn't hurt them.
They hurt you.

They fucked up
the relationship.

Therefore,
there's no need for *you*

to try

to fix things

if they're not willing
to fix it

themselves.

WHEN YOU ARE ALMOST HOME
THE FLOWERS BEGIN TO SPEAK TO
YOU

You're getting closer.

Don't overstress it.
Don't *overthink* it.

Just follow it.

You're almost there.
You're almost home.

Stop waiting for them
to change.

After all the chances
you've given them.

Nothing has changed.

They go back
to hurting you.

To not giving a fuck.

They're not going
to change.

Unless you change.

And realize...
That.

You.
Must.
Move on.

WHEN THE MEDALS AROUND YOUR NECK SPEAK FOR THEMSELVES

I'm happy
you moved on.

You deserve
a medal for that.

An award.
A round of applause

for putting up
with the bullshit

BUT

finding the courage
to let

that shit go.

WHEN YOUR TRUTH BECOMES YOUR WORD THEN YOU MUST LEARN TO LET THEM GO

Never give someone
the silent treatment.

Let them know
how you feel.

Let your voice
be heard.

Felt.
Fuck that.

Life is too short
to stay quiet.

Too short
to hold your tongue.

Speak your truth.

Even if

it hurts you.
Let others know
what's in your heart.

Even if
you don't know

where
to begin.

WHEN YOU THINK OF THEM AND REMEMBER WHY YOU LET THEM GO IT IS OKAY TO BE REMINDED OF THIS

It's okay
to think of them

while you're moving on.
While you're healing.

You're allowed
to break a little

even if
you left them

and did
the right thing.

THESE TYPE OF THINGS DO NOT HAPPEN WHEN THEY ARE *THE ONE* THESE TYPE OF THINGS SHOULD NOT BE PART OF YOUR STORY WITH THEM

If they were
really *"the one"*

then you wouldn't be
spending

so many
sleepless nights

overthinking
about why

they're gone.

THE PERSON IN THE MIRROR IS YOU AND IT HAS ALWAYS BEEN YOU NO ONE CAN CHANGE THAT

You were happy
before them.

You were good.
You were enough.

And you will be
after them.

You just have
to remember

what it was like
to love yourself.

That's all.

WHEN YOUR HEART CRAWLS OUT OF THE GRAVE IT BRINGS A WHOLE LOT OF MEMORIES WITH IT

The truth is

it only hurts
because you still care.

And you still care
because deep down inside

you still love them.
And there's nothing

realer
than that.

WHEN THE PHONE DOES NOT RING OR GET PICKED UP AND STAYS IN THE SAME PLACE YOU KNOW WHAT YOU HAVE TO DO

No one
is ever

too busy
to make time for you.

The sad truth is
they're either

seeing someone else
or

they just don't care.

Or

they're just not
that into you.

That's all.

WHEN IT IS AS SIMPLE AS BREATHING YOU KNOW YOU ARE MEANT TO REACH THE SKY

You're a flower.
And you're outgrowing

everything

that brings you down.
And everything

that hurts.

WHEN YOUR HEART IS HEAVIER THAN THE DOOR YOU KNOW WHICH ONE YOU CAN MOVE

Don't beg them
to stay.

Be the type of person
who holds the door

for them
and wishes them

the best.

WHEN YOU DO ALL THE HEAVY LIFTING YOU ARE BOUND TO SLIP AND FALL AND BREAK TO PIECES

Relationships are hard.

They take work.
They take effort.

They take time
and patience.

But make sure
you're not the only one

who's giving them all of that.
Make sure it's mutual.

Fifty fifty.

Make sure
they're just as involved

as you are.

This

is the only way
it'll work.

WHEN WE ARE ADDICTED TO BROKEN THINGS BROKEN PEOPLE AND BROKEN PLACES THIS IS A PART OF US WE WILL NEVER UNDERSTAND

That's just
how things are

sometimes.

We are drawn
to what breaks us.

To what destroys us.
To the people

who ignore us.

And to the ones
we need more from.

But it all stems
from the lack

of something.

And maybe
that's why
you keep chasing
the wrong people.

Maybe you were exposed
to pain

at a young age
and maybe

that's why you cope
with what hurts

so eloquently.

But it doesn't have
to be this way.

You don't need

to feel it
so regularly.

That feeling of desperation
and emptiness

is not your friend.
And just because
you are familiar with pain

doesn't mean
it's okay.

Doesn't mean
that this part

of your relationship
is normal.

That's not love, love.

That's attachment.
And it's not

what you need.
But it's what you want.

And I get it.
I really do.

We are drawn
to the people

who hurt us.

Naturally, too.

It's one of those things
we can't control.

One of those things
we want more of.

One of those things
we fight so hard

to figure out.

To fix.
But sooner or later

you are going to have to
make a decision.

Because

you can't live your life
like this.

You can't live
your life
unsure of love.

You have to find ways
to liberate yourself.

Find those little moments
where you feel

completely free.

And learn from them.
And let go

of all of that attachment.

Let go
of all of that pain.

That's not love, love.

And that's not normal.

Regardless
if you're used to it

or not.
Regardless
if it's the only thing you know.

That's not love, love.

You know what it is.
And deep down inside

you know
it is not this.

You can do better.
You can start over.

You can pick yourself...
and be free.

WE ALL WANT SOMEONE LIKE THIS WE ARE ALL SEARCHING FOR SOMEONE AND SOMETHING REAL

I just want
to meet someone

who's real.

Someone who speaks
their mind

but knows
how to respect me

and others.

Someone who's firm
but honest.

Someone who
doesn't beat around the bush

and lie

about everything.

Who knows
how to stay loyal.

Who doesn't fuck around
with people's hearts.

WHEN YOU ARE IN A TOXIC RELATIONSHIP YOU BEGIN TO THINK EVERYTHING IS YOUR FAULT

How naive was I.

Because one of the saddest things
I have ever done

was convince myself
to stay.

To convince myself
to give you

another chance.

And to convince myself
you'll change.

And without you
convincing me

to do so.

I believed in you that much.
And I wanted it to work

that much.

And sadly,
all you ever did

was blame me
for all the fuck ups.

And you had me believing it
at one point.

But it was all you.

I was just that blind.
I was just

that in love.

My only question is,
did I really deserve

all of that pain?

And why did I put
myself through it...

when I knew
from the very beginning

it wasn't worth
my time.

WHEN YOU CANNOT SEEM TO FIND THE RIGHT WORDS YOU MAKE YOUR OWN WORDS AND YOU DEFINE WHAT YOU FEEL AND FIND SOMETHING BEYOND WHAT YOU EXPECTED

Love
is when two people

feel the same way
about each other

and neither of them
have any recollection

of how it started.
Of how it began.

Love is two people
knowing how much

they care.

Without having

to remind each other

constantly.

Without making each other
feel left out.
Love is when
two people

just know.

When they understand
each other without the use

of words.

When they
speak their own language

and no one else
seems to get it

but them.

Love is two people
who stay.

Who form a bond
as they go on.

Who can't seem
to make sense
of their own lives
without each other.

Love is kind.

Two people being patient
with each other.

Two people
giving one another
time.

Their own precious time.

Every precious moment
that could be spent

doing something else.

Love is two people
growing together.

Giving each other guidance.
Giving each other

the kind of spark
that sets their souls
on fire.

Love is showing it.
That you care.

That you appreciate.
That you are willing

to sacrifice anything
to make the relationship work.

Love is two people.
Two hearts.

Two souls.
Two bodies.

Fusing.
Together.

Feeling what the other feels.
Knowing what the other knows.

And never doubting
any of it.
Always pushing
for greatness.

Together.

Always seeking
a little more.

WHEN YOU FIND IT HOLD ON TO IT YOU MAY NEVER GET ANOTHER CHANGE AT IT AGAIN

It is not
that people are fake.

It is just
that people do not care

about each other.

Nowadays
it is hard

to find someone
who is real.

Someone who cares.
Someone who really

wants to help.

To change someone else's life.
That is a rare thing.

When you find it.
Hold on to it.

Nurture it.
Let it grow

in the palm of your hands.
In the depths

of your heart.

In the corners
of your soul.

It is a beautiful thing
to experience.

The real connection
between people.

Let it bloom.

We are all
deserving

of this kind of friendship.
Of this kind of love.
Sometimes you just
have to open yourself up

and let things be.

Let things
make you feel

at home.

THIS MIGHT BE THE REALEST THING I HAVE EVER WRITTEN

You act
like you don't care

but you do.
And that

my dear
is your greatest

downfall.

WHEN PEOPLE BECOME STATUES THEY BECOME HEAVIER THAN THE WORLD

Love is not hard.

People are hard.
Hard to understand.

Hard to hold on to.
Hard to let go of.

Hard to love.
And hard to forget.

WHEN YOU LOVE THEM BUT LOVE YOURSELF FIRST IT IS NOT SELFISH IT IS A MIRACLE

I loved you.

I really did.
But I had

to take care of myself.
I had

to put everything
and everyone aside

for my own sake.

So when I said
it was not you
that it was me

I meant it.

I just couldn't be there for you.
I couldn't

give you what you deserved.
What you wanted
from me.

I couldn't make
you laugh anymore.

I couldn't brighten
your day.

Or make your life
a little easier.

I was
going through too much shit.

I had to get away.

It's just.
I couldn't love you

the way you needed
to be loved

because I needed

to love myself first.

I needed
to find myself first.

Find the things
that made me happy.

That gave me peace.

That spoke to my soul.
And stirred it.

I wanted to love you.
I wanted to be there for you.

But I couldn't.
A piece of myself

was missing.

And I just wanted
to be honest with you.

It was never you.
It was me.

I just hope

you understood that.
And I hope...

you never took things
the wrong way.

WHEN THE THINGS THEY SAID BECOME GHOSTS THEY FOLLOW YOU AROUND FOREVER

That's the thing.
No matter how much

time passes
it is some of the things

you said
that haunt me

the most.

WHEN YOU GIVE FLOWERS YOU RECEIVE THEM BACK AND EVERYTHING HAS BEEN SAID AND UNDERSTOOD

Remember.

Your life
should revolve around those
who stay.

Around those
who genuinely want

to love you.

Those
who genuinely care.

Forget the ones
who break their promises.

Forget the ones
who show you

no compassion.
No loyalty.

It's harsh to say.

And it hurts
to think about.

But you have to give
all your energy

to those
who are real with you.

Drink to those
lasting relationships.

Cherish them.

Hold them.
And make it count.

You never know
when you will see them last

until that day comes.

Remind them
of how much

you need them.

Of how much
you care.

Remind them
before it's too late.

Do it every moment
you can.

Because one day
it will be

your last chance
to do so.

And you won't even know it
it will be

too late.

WHEN YOU SAY FUCK THE WORLD DO NOT ASK MY FOR SHIT EVERYTHING YOU HAVE YOU NEED TO WORK HARD FOR IT

Do what you love.

And *fuck*
everything else.

Love who you want
to love.

And *fuck*
their opinions.

Fuck their criticisms.

You deserve to live
your life

the way you want
to live it.

Chase

who you want.

Be
who you want.

Dress how you want.
Speak what's in your heart.

Worship
what you believe in.

Be kind to others.

And *fuck* everything else.

Fuck the drama.
The pain.

The hate.
The media manipulation.

Fuck that.

Life is too short
to die wishing

you had done
a little more.

Sorry for my language
but fuck that, too.

Sometimes you have to fuck
the world

and everything
that pisses you off

to move forward.

Sometimes
you just have to

to get what you need.
And not

what you want

TO REMIND THEM EVERY CHANCE YOU GET IS A BLESSING WITHIN ITSELF

And just in case
I don't see you

in the morning.

Just in case
we don't speak.

I want you to know
that at this very moment

you are significant.

I want you to know
that you are loved.

And there is nothing
anyone can do

to change that.

I love you.
I love you.
I love you.

And I just

want to make sure
you know

how I feel.

WHEN YOU DON'T TAKE THE EASY PATH THE HARDEST ROUTE IS THE MOST REWARDING

I don't want
to have

to figure things out.

I don't want
to have

to overanalyze everything
you say.

Everything you do.

I want you
to love me

just as much
as I love you.

I want you
to show me

with action.
To act on it.

To not hold anything back.

I don't want you
to be afraid

to show me
what's in your heart.

I don't want you
to be shy.

Showing me
what you feel

is beautiful.

Your feelings
are beautiful.

And I don't want
to spend

a lifetime

trying to figure it out.
I love you now.

And tomorrow
and the next day.

But I need you
to trust me

with your heart.

I need you
to know

that I'll always have
your best interest

in mind.

I don't want to see you
go through hell again.

I just want *us*
to be okay.

But in order

to do so.
You have to know
with all your heart

that I am here for you.
That I am going to stay.

That I am not going
to fuck around with you.

No matter what.

Thank you for reading. And thank you for being a part of my journey... Of our journey.

Made in United States
Orlando, FL
24 November 2022

24948569R00125